Desiree Davidson

I0487225

Desiree's

Just

SEX!

Desiree

Davidson

Desiree Davidson

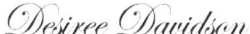

Desiree Davidson

Worldwide-Erotica

<u>Desiree's Just SEX!</u>

Desiree Davidson

DEDICATION

In remembrance of our Hunter,
Friend and Story Teller:

Gary V. Kieffer

We Will Always Remember You.

Desiree
Davidson

Desiree Davidson

CONTENTS

Desiree Davidson

Victoria's First Visit

to a

Nude Beach

It was the first time in their five year marriage that Franz and Victoria had taken a summer vacation and this first one was not what she expected it to be. They had only been down to the beach once just down from the house when he got a call on his cell phone and he announced that he had to go to Europe for two weeks -- something terribly important had come up and he had to attend a meeting of the partners of his investment bank. They gathered up their things and returned to the beach house and Victoria helped Franz pack.

She was already lonely and longed for him. His departure in the taxi cab was so soon that they hadn't made love – not even a quickie. She had one passionate kiss to keep her – Franz was a good kisser but he was magnificent in bed. Victoria had agreed to marry him after making love to him only one time. Both he and Victoria were highly sexed individuals and they were a perfect match for each other.

Victoria spent the afternoon sunning on the deck of the beach house. This part of the beach was private for the high end beach hours clustered together in a group of five. She noted that there didn't seem to be any beach activity up toward the other houses.

Victoria liked people and she was beginning to think that they had made a mistake in renting this isolated beach house. The house was beautiful and elegant and the beach was white sugar sand. She wasn't seeing anyone all afternoon so she resolved tomorrow to walk down the beach in the other direction and see if there was more activity.

She did not sleep well. Quite bluntly she was lonely and needed a good fuck and a nice round of those wonderful orgasms Franz helped her reach.

Victoria came in the night just thinking about sex.

Morning came and she had a fitful night. She fixed a light breakfast and then took a shower.

Rubbing herself dry brought her near orgasm but she just couldn't quite make it over the top!

Victoria put on her black bikini. It was in sharp contrast to her light blond natural hair.

She took her bag and packed a beach throw and a black blouse and pants, and then she added some snacks and water. She was ready to go exploring.

She took the stairs down from the deck to the beach and began to walk down the beach away from the beach houses. She went about half a mile and there was a sign that announced it was a nude beach ahead. Victoria had gone topless on the beaches of Europe but she had never been to a nude beach. She stood at the sign and considered what she should do. She needed the company of people so she made a compromise. She took her bikini top off and put it in her bag and sat off down the beach. Soon she came on an older man who was wearing trunks and there was an older woman in the water who appeared to be nude but she was too far away to be absolutely sure.

Victoria continued down the beach and saw a young man coming up the beach. As he drew near there was no doubt that he was nude – he had a very prominent dick and balls and he was becoming erect as he approached. She didn't mind. Seeing a man looking at her and getting erect was the highest compliment she could ever receive. She was 29 years old and could still turn on a 19 year old passing her on the beach.

Victoria came to a cliff area and there was a grotto shadowed from the sun. She didn't like to get too much skin since her husband didn't like her to have a full tan – he just wanted a healthy glow. She noticed that the pre afternoon temperature was a little cooler than she had anticipated. She would have put on her clothes but there was a fire pit and wood in the grotto. She decided to build a fire. Very quick the chill was taken off the grotto and Victoria stretched out on her beach throw. She was tired from her fitful sleep of the night and with the sound of the crashing waves she fell asleep.

She awoke and realized that there was a man – she judged about 25 – standing near her and his cock was fully erect and quite simply - magnificent. He was saying in broken English that he would like to take her. He was Brazilian and had beautiful brown skin. His body was very muscled and well proportioned. She understood that he wanted to fuck her and eventually she realized that he was encouraging her to remove her bikini bottom.

Victoria considered him and could feel her pussy tingle. He was about 9 inches long and very thick and had huge balls. Now she knew why her intuition had told her to put her diaphragm in. She decided -- she would fuck this young man -- she deserved the release. Victoria removed her bikini bottom and called the young Brazilian stud to her.

Manuel knelt between her legs and Victoria took his cock and guided the big head into her soaked pussy. He fucked her long and hard. The skin of his cock felt good as he stroked in and out of her cunt and played with her breasts. He was growing near the end. She lifted her long legs and wrapped them around his brown back as his cock began to shoot sperm into her blonde pussy. His balls were full of sperm and he filled Victoria. This was the first White woman he had ever fucked and he wanted to give her everything he had.

He pulled out of Victoria and she was so excited that she wished they could do it again so she could come. She communicated her desire to Manuel and in 10 minutes he was hard again. As they were fucking again Victoria came from his thick dick providing stimulation to her clit.

13

As she was coming, she realized that another man about 30 and White was watching her and growing fully erect. Manuel pulled out of her and Victoria sat up on the beach throw and felt his cum seeping from her pussy.

Rick approached her and complimented her on the show and volunteered his own services. He spoke English and was vacationing from Ohio and heard the Legend of the Grotto at the hotel and had to come and see if it were true.

Victoria said, "Legend?"

Rick explained -- you know -- a woman presenting herself here will receive anyone asking to make love.

Victoria didn't reply, but in her mind she was planning to stay the rest of the day and the evening and receive all who came.

It was the biggest sexual experience she had ever had.

Desiree Davidson

Double Entry Accounting

Stan and I were fellow hunters and had occasionally hunted girls together when we were young. We were talking one day about my wife being really attracted to him. He said if I gave him permission to seduce Desiree, then I could have his girlfriend, Susan. I agreed. My wife called Susan 'Wild Thing' primarily for her fluffy wild blonde hair style that she had when the four of us were seated together at a school banquet. My cock was hard the whole time I was near her. Her perfume or was it natural pheromone made me want to fuck her right there. A few weeks later I found my wife had correctly tagged her, but for sex-- the girl loved it and wanted everything a man (or men) could give her. Susan was totally open to the idea of entertainment with me and was available the next Saturday afternoon. Coincidentally I would be free, because my wife was going shoe shopping with her sister and her mother.

I went to Stan's house at the appointed time of 1 pm. Stan's car was not in the driveway, but Susan's was. I rang the bell and much to my pleasant surprise Susan opened the door and invited me in. Susan was wearing an open front beige lingerie jacket and matching bikini panties--the sheerness of the material did nothing to hide her beautiful body. The top and bottom had little pale blue ribbon ties. Susan was a doll! At 6' she was only two inches shorter in height than me. She had on bone colored high heels at the time, so actually with the heels and a good six inches of teased hair, she was taller than me.

Stan told me she was 25. I was 26 at the time of our first sexual encounter. She would be the 1,750th sex partner of my life. She was going to be fun. Susan had beautiful long legs and I could already envision them wrapped around my back (with her high heels still on) while I fucked her face to face and looked into her pretty grey eyes. She probably was a true blonde when she was a child; for even now the cover of her mons was very light blonde brown.

Susan invited me to sit down on   the sofa. We talked a little while.
She said, "Eric, I work for a credit card company in Accounting. What do you do?"

"Well, I returned to college after a stint with the Navy and I am finishing my degree in Electrical Engineering." I told her.

"She had attended all the school she wanted," she told me.

"When I was through with high school in Oklahoma City I completed my formal education for all time. It's hard to have lots of fun in high school when you have to do so much work," she said.

I said, "I grew up right here in the Tecumseh-Shawnee area."

As we continued to talk, my cock was straining to get out of my pants and her big firm nipples strained equally against the sheer fabric of her top. I thought both of us were adequately acquainted and I began to softly stroke her soft legs. With my other hand, I touched her warm face and told Susan how beautiful she was. I moved forward and kissed her warm, wet, full lips softly and she kissed back but

16

much more firmly. We continued to kiss as she carried me beyond soft to passionate then to ultra-passionate open mouth kisses. As we kissed I continued to stroke her long ivory legs.

After about 15 minutes I stood up and undressed and turned to face her.

Susan said, "Wow! You're almost as big as Stan and he's huge."

I returned to sit by her and placing a finger to her lips I said, "I think you will find my cock much easier for oral and other activity."

I reached for the little bows holding the top closed and I untied them. This allowed me to feel the soft, warm skin of her breasts and to directly fondle her large pink nipples.

"They are lovely," I said. I leaned over and tongued and suckled them.

She said, "That feels great, keep doing it--Stan never pays enough attention to my breasts!"

I did keep doing it after she stood up and let me take the jacket off and then her panties. Then she sat down by me. Now we were nude together.

I said, "Susan, I am about to burst to have you, are you ready for sex?"

"Yes," she said, as she led me to the bedroom.

She lay down and her beautiful, wispy blonde hair covered the pillow.

I was too inflamed to wait. I moved over her. My cock was fully hard and my balls were ready to plant my sperm in this pretty prize.

Susan took my cock in her hand and placed me into her delicious, tight, wet pussy. (It made me wonder how much fore play she had to have with

Stan before sex, for he is significantly thicker then I am and he could have never entered her now.)

I moved into her and her cunt felt great. Fully in her, I leaned down and kissed her full firm ivory breasts and flicked her big pink nipples with my tongue, as I built her excitement.

Susan said, "I love the way you make love to my breasts--you're the only man I've been with who does that. Swirl your tongue around my areola some more."

Susan said, "I'm adjusted to your big cock now and I want to be fucked."

Her pussy was wet and very tight on my cock so I began to take long slow strokes. As she relaxed I sped up the pace of my thrusts in her pretty body. Susan's clit was very prominent and very shortly the classy little girl started coming on me as we continued to fuck. She continued to come in waves and in a few minutes I couldn't hold back and I joined her and shot stream after stream of hot cum into her pretty body. When we had both finished, I pulled out of her and held her and kissed her in the afterglow of a beautiful sexual experience.

About thirty minutes had elapsed since we started. I asked her to '69' with me. She was a great cock sucker and from the hard loud orgasms, I believe I was proving I knew my way around her delicious cunt. I came in her mouth and I moved up and in a deep kiss, Susan gave my cum back to me. We continued to touch, fondle and kiss for a long time.

Then I asked Susan what sex position she would like to try.

Susan said, "I occasionally like anal sex, but Stan is so big I won't let him touch me that way. You're big but not so huge in thickness--I'd like to take you that way. "

We kissed and fondled for several more minutes, then I prepared her for entry.

I reached for my zippered pouch and got out lubricant for our next romp. I prepared her by opening her anus with my three lubricated fingers until I was sure she could take me comfortably. Then she lubricated my long hard cock. Her hands felt wonderful as she coated me and then briefly jacked me off.

Susan lay on her back and I took her beautiful long legs over my shoulders. I took my cock in my hand while supporting my weight on one arm and placed the swollen purple head against her relaxed anus. I gently moved in and slowly pressed past her sphincter muscle and completely entered her body to the full length of my cock.
Susan, "Are you comfortable?" I said.

"Eric, go ahead, I'm adjusted to your cock and it feels wonderful so deep in my ass."

I picked up the pace and in a short order my lovely long legged nymph was milking huge streams of cum out of my cock and balls.
Susan did not come with anal intercourse, so when we finished I lay between her long legs and tongued her clit. Shortly she was crying out in ecstasy as waves of orgasms swept over her body.

I went to the bath room and cleaned up, and returned with a warm washcloth to remove the lubricant that remained on Susan.

On my return, I had her kneel over my face with my head supported on a doubled pillow. I bathed her clit in licks and very shortly she was writhing as she came repeatedly to my flicking tongue. Susan finally satiated herself and moved off and lay down beside me. We both needed a break and we just lay for a long time just looking at each other. As a couple we fucked one more time in the face to face position. Almost two hours had elapsed when we heard Stan come in the front door.

I called out, "Did you come to watch?"
Stan replied, "I'd love to but I need your help. I'd like to watch as a participant."

He went on to say Susan had never been double penetrated (ass and cunt) by two men. "I thought we could change that while you're here." he said.

Susan wanted to try it also. We went about the logistics of it. I would lie on my back and facing toward my feet, Susan would impale her body on my cock. Stan would then lay her back on my body and then as I held her, he would enter her pussy. That is exactly what happened and the result proved exactly what I had experienced in the past with other woman, Susan came so heard her cries of passion proved that she was "Wild Thing." She was a delicious fuck and she really came unglued when Stan began to come in her cunt and then I joined in her ass--she was amazing--what a delicious sex partner!

Stan did seduce my wife Desiree, and I was with his beautiful Susan some 21 other times.

On the Edge

She went to the pool late in the day. There were a handful of kids and their mothers and two young Black men. Her husband was on a trip and to be perfectly honest, she was horney. She had used her vibrator and come several times, but what she really needed was her husband's long thick dick to make her come while he fucked her.

The kids and their mothers thinned out and as the sky grew dusky but before the pool lights came on, she was left alone with the two young men. They were 19 to 22 she thought, but it was hard to judge the age of young Black men. She was 40 but looked 30. Her light green bikini set off her blonde hair and did little to cover her large firm breasts. The bottom showed lots of cheek and she had trimmed her blonde pussy hair so there was not a single strand peeking out from the tiny bikini bottom.

Rachel was floating upright in the deep end of the pool and there was a flotation chair left there, so she took it in tow and swam one handed toward the shallow end of the pool. As she passed she bumped into one of the two Black men.

Rachel said, "I'm sorry – I hope that didn't hurt.

Jamaal said, "No, Let us get that for you" and took the chair and lifted it out of the pool and left it at the edge.

Rachel had used the chairs to float in the pool a number of times and they were quite comfortable to recline in.

Jamaal went back to Denel and Janet came over to thank them for helping her.

Jamaal and Denel were wearing swim trunks that clung to their bodies. It was somehow gratifying to still look good enough and exude sexiness enough at 40 that both young men were showing obvious signs of getting hard – pool shrinkage was obviously not a factor here.

Rachel was on the deeper side and took their arms to keep her afloat. At 5'2", 110 pounds and naturally big busted she could float or she could stand, but only if the water was shallow enough. Rachel asked their names and told them hers and asked if they lived in the complex. They said they were visiting their friend and he had gone up to take care of some business but should be back soon. Rachel's cunt was on fire. She hadn't been fucked in four days and couldn't wait till her husband came home.

The sky was growing darker but it would be a while before the pool lights came on.

The men had been eying her big breasts and were both fully hard. She decided that she would have to initiate what she wanted. It was simple enough –

"Would you guys like to fuck me?" Rachel said.

There was silence for a long period and then each one confirmed they would love to give the pretty blond their big Black cocks.

Rachel told them to bring the floating chair back into the pool and both saw what she had in mind when she got into the chair with her legs open and dangling into the water. Denel pulled her bikini bottom from her legs and Jamaal pulled his trunks off and revealed a thick cock about 10inches in length.

He moved the chair out into the water to where his hungry Black dick was positioned at Rachel's cunt and Denel kept the chair steady in the water while his friend fucked her pretty White pussy.

Rachel said, "Take your time – be sure and come in me –don't pull out – your dick feels wonderful – I want to feel you come in me."
At the same time, Rachel began coming on his big Black dick and could only cry out in pleasure.

Jamaal came in Rachel flooding her womb with hundreds of millions of Black sperm. When he finished, he stepped aside and steadied the chair while Denel entered Rachel. He was very thick but only about eight inches in length.

Denel entered Rachel very easily thanks to her natural wetness and his friend going first and saturating her cunt with semen. Denel in only a few strokes had Rachel coming again. It was exciting to do something she had never done before --let a Black man fuck her. Rachel scooted down to get every stroke of this young Black stud. Denel was in a hurry and quickly began to dump his big Black balls into Rachel's little blonde cunt. Rachel longed for more fucking. Rachel's wish was granted -- there was another and almost as soon as Denel pulled out of her pussy their friend stepped between her legs and rapidly fucked her to orgasm with his long thick Black dick. Even a third was not enough. She moved off the chair into the water and streams of cum flowed out of her dilated cunt and floated away into the water.

One of the Black studs gave her the bikini bottom and steadied her while she slipped it back on.

23

He was the last to trunk up and finished just at the pool lights came on.

Rachel pulled each one's face to her and kissed them and told them what wonderful studs they were. Then she had a wicked thought and acted on it. She invited all three to her apartment to fuck them properly -- singularly and in combination.

Rachel was impaled with one Black dick in her cunt and one in her ass when her husband called. She told the one she was sucking off to get the cordless phone for her. She told her new Black friends to be very quite. Then she answered his call and told him she was doing good but missed him and wished she could have his cock right now. They flirted a while and then she quickly hung up because she was coming and crying out in pleasure from being doubled by two delicious Black dicks.

Party

Nick and Jill had never attended a sex party together before and it was something Nick wanted to do more than Jill.

Jill had taken thirty-three men as lovers during the first five years of their marriage and perhaps 75 men since she became sexually active at 13, and she wasn't sure she could refuse any man or woman at the party without Nick being disappointed. Besides she didn't like to use condoms and she was sure the men at the party would.

Nick had been with many women before and during their marriage. Indeed, Nick had fucked her best friend Susan, while she had taken Susan's husband in a couple-swap just last week.

Both Nick and Jill liked to watch each other with a new partner and that was what had made her decision final when Nick suggested a sex party, but that was not the main reason.

***

Jill got out of the tub just a few minutes after Nick stepped out of the shower. Jill thought, "My husband's a real stud -- look at the size of his balls and his thick 10-inch long cock. I love the feel of him coming in me. That reminds me; I better put my diaphragm in so I can take some man who wants to fuck me without a condom. She loved the feeling it gave her to feel her lover's semen spray into her body."

25

Jill was a lucky woman, she did have a wonderful sex partner in her husband, but it was always nice to take a new man on occasion.
Nick had gone into the bedroom. She got out of the foam filled tub and began to dry herself off. As she dried her c-cup breasts, she thought, "I wish my breasts were bigger, Nick was really impressed by Susan's d-cup breasts, and her greedy cunt was very impressed with Nick's big long cock."

Jill dried her cunt and then her long shapely legs. She had great legs, she thought, "Every one of the men she had fucked had told her so. They loved to have her wrap them around their muscled backs and draw their cocks into her wet, tight pussy."

Jill after thoroughly drying herself opened a drawer and took out her case and the spermicidal jelly and placed her diaphragm. She wished she could do without it, but Nick was firm that he wanted to be the father when she decided to become pregnant. She moved and confirmed that it properly covered her cervix – she was ready to fuck any man or men (she was curious about a gang bang – when she was sixteen she had let three football players fuck her repeatedly and it was fantastic – she couldn't believe how many times they had shot their cum into her body before she fucked them dry. She had not expressed this "curiosity" to Nick but it was the main reason she actually agreed to go to a party.

Jill, fully nude, walked into the bedroom and caught Nick just about to dress. She walked to him and stroked his quickly stiffening cock and told him she wanted to see his cock buried in lots of delicious cunts tonight – but when they got to the party she wanted him to fuck her first and then let her suck him

26

hard again as she sent him off ready for his next pussy. Nick liked the idea and told her that he would be taking the best pussy first. Nick continued and told her he wanted her to be totally free to do anything she wanted to do – this was her night to enjoy.

Jill asked him, "Anything?"

Nick replied, "Anything."

Nick's fingers found her swollen pussy lips and rapidly developing wetness and almost regretted giving her to other men, but both of them knew their lovers and sex adventures were what had kept their marriage exciting and vital – monogamy would have never worked for either of them.

***

Jill and Nick were greeted by the host and hostess and told that there would be 12 couples at the party but only 3 had arrived and there was going to be three single guests to even up the entertainment of the women. Both Jill and Nick were excited. The host directed them to a bedroom where they could change out of their clothes.

Nick waited for Jill and they walked to the party room and saw the three couples already paired off and fucking away.

There was lots of room on the mats and Nick and Jill took up a spot farthest away from the fucking couples. Jill lay down on her back and Nick moved between her legs and proceeded to kiss her and again tell her that he wanted her to do anything she wanted tonight. Then Jill took his hard cock in her hand and guided her husband's cock into her wet pussy. They fucked for about 10 minutes and then both she and Nick came together as he sprayed his hot sperm into her body.

While they were fucking several people had come in and settled into different combinations. Nick pulled out of her and he moved to lean against a couch and she moved to suck his cock. She was on her hands and knees and proceeded to suck Nicks cock hard. He was almost fully hard when he told her that there was a man behind her who wanted to fuck her. She continued to suck and mumbled OK. She felt fingers open her cum drenched labia and slide into her cunt to make sure she was ready. Next she felt a huge cock head pass her labia and begin to penetrate her – she could take him, but she wanted to see who was about to fuck her and told Nick so.

Jill looked around and saw the Blackest Black man she had ever seen and at that moment felt the biggest dick she had ever had begin to inch its way into her pussy. Nick moved out of the way and Jill and her Black stud moved together so she could rest her upper body on the cushion. Jill would later learn that the Black man fucking her was named Jerome. Right now it was enough for her to cry out excitedly – "God. You wonderful stud! Your dick feels great! Don't ever stop fucking me!" – Just as she began to come on his long thick Black dick.

Jill and Jerome fucked for about 15 minutes and Jill was having wave after wave of orgasms convulse her body as Jerome's dick and balls convulsed and filled her body with the first Black sperm she had ever had.

Jerome pulled out of her and helped her to the mat because her legs were weak and shaking from

28

her orgasms. She lay down on her back with her beautiful long blond hair splayed out over the mat. It was then that she saw her husband watching her and everyone at the party gathered around the watch the Black stud fuck the beautiful sexy blonde. Jerome's semen was gathered in the blond patch of her pussy and left no doubt that she had taken him bare back. The crowd wanted more and so did she and Jerome – he was fully erect again. Jill wanted to do something. She wanted this amazing Black stud to have all of her.

Jill turned to Nick who was keeling by her. "I want something, she said. I want to let him have all of me."

Nick said, "Do anything you want Baby. What do you want to do?"

Jill said, "I want to take my diaphragm out and let his sperm enter all of me!

Jill really didn't hear what her husband said, but it really didn't matter for she was already taking her diaphragm out and handing it to Nick.

Jerome moved between her legs and his huge dick entered her again. He proceeded to fuck the pretty little blond bitch who wanted his sperm in her womb.

All the men and woman watched them fuck again and called out for Jill to come (which seemed to happen continuously on that beautiful big Black dick) and for Jerome to fill her with his hot sperm. The crowd stayed and watched Jill get fucked by the Black stud a third time, and then Jerome came in her and pulled out to quickly recover and take another woman who was hungering for his big Black dick.

Jill lay on the mat and caught her breath. Her husband moved between her legs and entered her and almost immediately came in her. By the time Nick was through with Jill, there were several men in line waiting to fuck her. Her gang bank with twelve White men and two other Black men (special guests) proceeded through the night and she could hardly walk when Nick came and told her she had had enough.

At home in a nice hot bubbly tub Jill relaxed and thought of the slut she had been – she wouldn't have changed a thing and certainly not her first Black stud or her gang bang.

Nick came in and laid her diaphragm on the bath edge.

Jill looked at it and wondered what her husband was thinking.

"Jill he said, "I don't want you to ever use this thing again. You can't possibly know how exciting it is to know that another man may be impregnating your wife!"

Jill reached up and touched his face and said, "I think you may have enjoyed the party as much as I did. I'll always be unprotected when anyone fucks me just for you!

Nick said "I invited that Black stud you enjoyed so much to come to our house next Tuesday and fuck you again while I watch."

Jill said, "That's wonderful. Can I fuck him anytime he wants me?

Jill, my baby doll, you can wrap your pretty blonde pussy around that big Black dick anytime you want!

Desiree Davidson

Hot Tub Friends

Teresa and Mark kept their marriage alive and exciting by fulfilling each other's fantasy. It was Mark's turn to name the fantasy and Teresa would carry it out. She was very excited about the latest because she had grown curious about what she would find – there were so many stories and tales she had grown up with. Now at 28 she was going to find out the truth for herself. Mark wanted to watch while she fucked a Black Man!

Mark had done some scouting and found a nice hotel that seemed to be frequented by Black men traveling on business. The hotel had an indoor pool and next to it a small hot tub that would seat four. They checked in and took a walk around the hotel to decide how they would proceed with Teresa picking up a Black stud for Mark's fantasy.

Teresa decided she would wait until about 8 o'clock and see if a suitable man came to the hot tub. If that didn't work she would dress up and choose someone in the hotel bar to approach.

Teresa was a petite brunette and had just bought a skimpy bright red bikini that left nothing to the imagination. The top was unlined and her big nipples stood out proudly. The bottom was a thong and hardly enough to cover her trimmed patch of brown hair. Teresa looked at herself in the mirror and Mark whistled at this first view of her new bikini.

Mark said, "God you are a walking "fuck me sign' in that outfit."

Teresa was pleased. That's exactly what she hoped it would be because she was determined she was going to fulfill Mark's fantasy and her secret curiosity tonight.

They went down to the pool and sure enough there were two good looking muscle Black men in the hot tub. Mark and Teresa joined them and Because of the small size of the hot tub, Teresa was right next to the man the other called Devon. Devon was about 30 and must have worked out because he was ripped.

Teresa hoped the two Black men had just met and were not together, because leaning her leg against his under the bubbling water made a noticeable bulge in his swim trunks.

Teresa was blessed with luck because the other man got up and called back "Maybe I'll see you tomorrow – I've got to go get dressed and take my wife out dancing."

When they had come in, Teresa had laid their towels and belongings on a lounger. She got out of the tub and purposely bent over so Devon would see her exposed ass and barely covered pussy. Then she straightened up and let him see her just right body. The she returned to the hot tub and sat down between her husband and Devon.

Devon said "What are your names. They introduced themselves and Teresa noted that Devon's bulge was significantly larger than it had been before she put on her little show.

Teresa asked if he had brought his wife with him too. He said no and went on and said he was divorced.

32

Teresa purposely moved closer to him and again stroked her leg across his leg and immediately after that reached through the bubbling water and grasped his swollen dick through the trunks. Immediately she said I'd like to take "this" in my pussy while my husband watches.

Devon looked at Teresa in a long pause and then asked where.

Teresa replied, "In our room."

Devon said to Mark, "Are you OK with this man?"

Mark said, "Both of us want it."

"OK Devon, said, "I'm ready for it.

With that Teresa got out of the tub and led the party in drying off and led Devon to their room with Mark bringing up the rear. Once in the room, Devon took Teresa's bikini off and had her fully naked and then dried her off and then he took his trunks off and freed a magnificent 12 in long, very thick Black cock. Teresa grabbed the towel and dried his muscled buttocks and spent a long time drying his cock and balls. Mark had dried himself and had settled down in a chair to watch the action. He was slowly stroking his own smaller cock as he watched his wife dry that Black monster. He was waiting in excited anticipation of seeing Devon fuck his wife for the first time.

Teresa had just gone off birth control pills and had fucked several men she had desired in the last couple of months without condoms so she was going to give all of herself to this Black man as well.

She was actually fantasizing that this Black stud would impregnate her. It built the excitement ever higher and Mark and she had talked about unprotected sex and he was fine with the idea that another man might impregnate her and it only made his fantasy hotter when he thought a Black man might do it. On questioning him about his fantasy a few days before her learned that possibly being impregnated by a Black man was a big part of it. She just wanted a baby and Mark didn't seem capable of giving her one.

Teresa finished drying Devon and stood up dropping the towel to the floor. Devon bent to kiss her and she received it open mouth. Then he picked her up and carried her to the bed and lay her down well into the king size bed. Then he joined her and sucked her breasts as his long fingers gauged the readiness of her pussy for his big cock. Teresa lubricated rapidly and opened to his fingers. Her cunt was on fire and she wanted to be fucked and told him so.

Devon said, "You sexy slut, you might be ready to fuck a White man but you're not relaxed enough to take my cock."

Teresa insisted that he fuck her now and he moved between her legs. He called Mark over and had him hold his cock while he gently pushed just inside her. When Mark turned loose he was firmly in the opening of her cunt and she was begging that he fuck her; so he gave a hard thrust and penetrated her six inches. Teresa screamed in pain at the same time a wave of orgasms rushed across her body.

"Give me all you got," she cried. He did – bottoming out with the head of his cock pushed snuggly against her tilted cervix.
Devon was letting her relax to his size and she was still having orgasm with him just staying in her.

"This White bitch is so sexy, I could come in her right now," he thought. Then suddenly his balls contracted and he spewed his creamy cum all over her cervix and uterus.

Teresa, felt him cum in her and cried out, "Don't stop fucking me. I've got to have your cock in me."

Her pleading encouraged him to recover quickly and he began to stroke in and out of her pussy wondering how many orgasms this hot little White bitch could have. She was in the throes of pleasure constantly and with her legs wrapped around his back he wasn't going anywhere and certainly did not want to leave this sweet pussy.

About 10 minutes passed and he came in her again filling her body with his hot cum.

Raining

I was on a business trip and decided to go down in the Italian neighborhood of Cleveland, Ohio and find an authentic Italian restaurant. I drove down the narrow streets and saw one I'd like to try but all the street parking was full and I had to park eight blocks away and walk back. When I walked in there was an attractive woman asking to be seated at a table for one.

In those moments she stood talking to the hostess I decide I wanted her.
It was late fall and the weather was variable. She had on a green knit sheath dress that hugged her curves. On close examination it was obvious that there were no bra or panty lines visible. That intrigued me.

She had somewhat of a square face but she was quite attractive in her own unique way. Her hair was medium wheat colored blond and due to the varying shades of the primary color it was highly likely that she was a natural.

She wore spike heel boots and she was without hose. The ivory color of her face was repeated in her bare legs.

She was by anyone's measure a woman to be pursued.
The hostess took her away and seated her in the back of the restaurant and then returned to greet me. I told her I needed a table for one, but could she seat me near the beautiful woman she seated before?

She smiled and said "I will be happy too; this was a place for lovers."

She placed me one table over and seated me in a position so I was facing Toni as I would soon find her name by introducing myself and she in return giving me hers. She was open to conversation and I asked if I could join her at her table and she agreed.

The waiter came and we were occupied for a few minutes, but after he left we began to get to know each other. She was on a business trip too and had to park a number of blocks away just as I had done. The sun was setting and by the time we would be through it would be dark. I asked her if I could walk her to her car after our meal and she said that would be nice.

All during the meal we got to know each other better and as we were having dessert and coffee, I reached over and took her hand. Just touching her was electrifying. I decided to make my move as we walked to her car, but her show of interest in me led me to believe that making love to her was in my future.

I paid the check and we went out of the restaurant. In the night sky there were threatening storm clouds and lightning.

We held hands as we walked and suddenly the sky let loose with a torrential downpour. We were about four blocks from the restaurant and getting soaking wet. There was a small covered loading dock that opened on the street and we sought shelter there.

Toni leaned against the brick wall catching her breath and then she said come here. I did not have far to go to be in front of her. Toni took my face and pulled me down to kiss her. After the initial kiss it was totally blurred about who was initiating the next kiss, but there was no doubt about what followed. Toni said, "I want you to fuck me right here in the rain."

I reached for the hem of her sweater dress and pulled it up above her large firm breasts. She had huge nipples and absolutely perfect breasts. I started to bend to them with my mouth but Toni stopped me when she said, "I want you to fuck me now, there will be time for that later."

I moved slightly back and dropped my slacks and shorts and she lifted a leg around my hip and my throbbing cock entered her delicious pussy. I fucked her for only a few minutes and she began to come and kept coming until about ten minutes of fucking, when I shot stream after stream of come into her body. When her last orgasms subsided, I pulled out of her still almost fully erect.

Toni took my hard cock in her hand and she said, "I have to have more of this guy – he's wonderful and so big. Come with me to my hotel where we can continue this more comfortably."

As it turned out, her hotel just happened to be my hotel so loving her was easy.

When we got in her room, we stripped our wet clothes off and got into a hot shower together and got to know each other's bodies more completely. While we dried each other, Toni said, "Eric, I've never done anything like that, but in the movies it looks so sexually charged that I just had to try it"

"I'm glad you did," Eric replied, "Were you satisfied with your experience?"

Toni said, Satisfied for then, but now I need you to lay me down in that big, soft, king size bed and see how many times you can fuck me before morning."

Desiree Davidson

Anniversary Gift

His wife Anne had been a virgin when Dan married her. Dan on the other hand had more sex experience packed into his 22 year old life than could be believed. And he married a woman who valued fidelity almost above all other things. Dan was faithful and Anne was faithful for all their marriage, but Dan missed the old variety. Their 36th wedding anniversary was coming up and he always got to ask Anne for a present. Anne was beautiful an ageless woman of 58 years who looked to be in her early 40's.

By any man's judgment Anne was a sexy beautiful woman.

Dan asked for his gift choice and he was dumbfounded when she said yes.

Dan's fingers trembled as he wrote the ad soliciting a man for his wife – you see he'd always wanted to watch. Anne had placed no restrictions other than what she was willing to do to give Dan his anniversary present.

Dan returned to writing his advertisement. This was probably the only chance he'd get, so he might as well raise the stakes. "A young muscular man, well hung and willing to make love to Anne while he watched and joined in." were the words that flowed from his fingers. He knew this was far beyond what Anne had agreed to, but he had a feeling. He attached a seductive picture of Anne with the ad and closed down the computer. About three hours later he began to have second thoughts and decided to go to the computer and cancel his ad and replace it with the one Anne had agreed to. Much to his surprise there were already 37 replies from men who wanted his wife. He was amazed and decided to leave his ad alone.

He began to go though the replies and classify them as rejects, maybes and definitely. This process continued the next evening while Anne was out with a friend. He had to work fast for he had 739 replies. He thought he had enough so he was about to stop the ad when one last reply came through – he was a definite but Anne would never be with him in a million years. Dan would love to see it happen though.

The next day at work he spent his lunch hour going through the definite group and looking for the very best one – it still came down to the last man replying. "What would Anne do with him?" Dan thought. Probably not even what she had agreed to and certainly not what Dan would like to see her do with Ted.

The next day Dan called Ted and found they worked in the same building but for different firms. Neither had commitments so they met for lunch at a secluded restaurant where they could have a private conversation.

Dan was up front about the vast difference in sex acts Anne had agreed to and those in Dan's ad and Ted was made aware of one other potential problem. Ted agreed to the limited act and to what Dan really wanted because as he told Dan he could almost feel her riding his dick from just looking at her picture.

After Lunch they went in the men's room which conveniently had low privacy shields between urinals and Ted could quickly prove he as hung as was stated in his ad reply. Dan and Ted sat at the bar a minute and went over the details for next Sunday at the Four Seasons Hotel where the anniversary present was to be given. Dan would reserve two adjoining rooms so he and Ann could be getting ready for this meeting, while Ted undressed in the next room and could then just walk in when he heard the code word.

Sunday came and Ann and Dan went to the hotel room about 6 pm. Dan had rented the rooms and prepared the connecting rooms and left a card key at the front desk for Ted to pick up.

The rules were simple, Anne had agreed to wear a bikini bottom which tied at the side (Dan had insisted on the design and to leave her breasts exposed so the man Dan had selected could fondle them if he wanted. The other part of the anniversary gift would be that the man would be fully naked. All Dan told Anne was that the man's name was Ted and he was a muscular young man about 30 years younger than Dan and Ann and that he was the man Dan wanted her to be with. She with some reservation had agreed to satisfy a many years old desire of Dan that he get to watch her suck another man's cock and let him come in her mouth.

Dan undressed completely and watched Anne change out of street clothes and put on the red bikini bottom. Dan hoped it would be coming off too.

Anne turned the king size bed down and lay down. Dan joined her and they spent a long time kissing and fondling as if they were going to make love. Both Anne and Dan were anxious about the

41

coming event but the anxiety seemed to change to sexual excitement for both of them.

Dan maneuvered Anne to the middle of the big bed so he could be on one side and Ted could be on the other.

Dan used a sentence with the code word in it and Ted stepped into the room.

Anne said, "Oh my God!"

Dan for a second, thought that Anne's exclamation was because Ted was Black, but she continued and said, "Look how big he is!"

Ted was mostly flaccid when he'd walked in the room but seeing Anne's beautiful naked breasts and her mostly naked body, Ted went instantly hard as he walked to the bed where Anne was waiting for him. Ted lay down on the bed and turned on his side toward Anne who understood what he wanted. Anne moved down in the bed so her face was at his cock. He was long and thick – three of her finger wide and by her hands size on it at least twelve inches long. This was not unusual to Anne, her husband who was videotaping this anniversary gift was hung himself but somehow on this muscular black man his Black cock seemed even bigger.

Anne stroked him and the head of his cock swelled in anticipation and his huge balls moved in anticipation as well.

Dan was super excited watching his pretty ivory skinned wife examining this Black stud he'd found for her. He was ok with Anne's rules, but he wished for more. Regardless he continued to videotape this special anniversary so he could relish it in the years to come – he really thought Anne would cooperate only this once.

Anne began to lick the dark plum colored head of Ted's cock and she found it excited her more than she had ever felt with Dan. As she licked she cradled Ted's ball. Just one filled her hand. "He definitely was a sex machine," she thought.

Ted thought Anne couldn't possibly be 59 as Dan had said. He had been with many women and Anne looked to be 40 to 45. He was extremely excited and hoped he could take this beautiful White woman completely – but he was willing to follow Anne's rules.

While Ted was reflecting, Anne had taken the head of his cock in her mouth and more excitement was building if that was possible.
Dan videotaped in close up when Anne had taken the Black's cock in her mouth. He pushed her blond hair back to get a clear shot as her red lipstick smeared lip prints on the black Shaft.

Time seemed to be standing still but in reality Anne had been sucking Ted for more than ten minutes. Ted had previously curved his back so he could fondle her beautiful breasts and large pink nipples. Now he straightened his back, his balls tightened and his hot cum erupted in Anne's mouth. She couldn't swallow it all - there was just too much - and much spilled out on the sheets. She did purposely keep a mouth full though, as Ted finished with her.

Anne motioned for Dan and he came to her and she French kissed him filling his mouth with Ted's hot cup. She had wondered what he would do and was very surprised that the experience caused her husband to shoot his come all over her abdomen as she gave a few strokes to his erect cock.

Dan went back to videotaping because somehow he thought there was more to come.

Anne lay down by Ted and as he touched her breasts She led him into soft kisses and then more passionate. Anne was making up her mind about two things 1) would she let a man other than her husband 2) would she let this handsome black man fuck her! She made her decision.

"Dan, come here and take my bikini bottom off."

It was a command that the two men quickly understood. As Dan untied the sides and pulled the bikini bottom away from his beautiful wife's body, he realized Anne was going to give him what he really wanted.

Anne lay on her back with her legs open and asked Dan to insert his fingers in her pussy to be sure she was ready to take this Black stud he'd brought her. He complied and found her wet and ready to give herself to Ted. Ted moved between her legs as he was fully recovered from the oral sex and was ready to fuck her. She took his huge cock and placed the head of his cock into the swollen lips of her pussy.

Dan was busily videotaping again and his 58 year old cock was far from growing hard again.

Ted slowly inserted his cock into her and Anne was on the verge of coming from just letting this Black man fuck her. Suddenly she lifted her long legs and encircled the stud's back and fully impaled her cunt on his cock.

She was vaginally orgasmic and almost always came with her husband thrusting in her for ten minutes, but now what she was doing had a forbidden sense about it as she impaled herself on a Black man

44

and immediately she shuddered in orgasm and cried out in pleasure as the powerful waves of pleasure swept over her.

Ted began to thrust into this beautiful White woman. Since her husband was well hung, her vagina was wet and tight and the beautifully little blond bitch was coming just from being fully penetrated by him and now as he thrust into her she was having even stronger orgasms.

Anne kept herself fit and by tightening her muscles just right she could force her husband to come in her – right now she wanted this Black man's sperm in her and she began to practice her art all the time reveling in orgasms.

Ted could feel what she was doing to his cock and he was delighted. Soon he could no longer resist and he began to pump his sperm into this sexy little bitch. He wished he could impregnate her but he realized that day was probably long gone.

Dan was taping everything and was delighted with his anniversary gift.

Anne was delighted that she followed her instincts and fucked this wonderful Black stud. The question now in her mind was how many times could she fuck him before she had to give him up.

They fucked three more times and felt like more. Dan was out of tape so he left Anne and Ted alone while he went out of the hotel to purchase more. The time allowed Ted and Anne to be alone and fuck again – this stud was insatiable and so was she. Now they could tell each other how they felt about each other – each wanted the other as often as possible.

Dan returned and continued to videotape until in an interlude, Anne asked him to stop. She said he

45

had received enough of his anniversary gift, but she had not.

"Dan, she said, "I'm having a wonderful time with Ted and … Well; I want to spend the rest of the night with him. I want to be alone with him."

Dan smiled and then kissed her and said, "I'll just watch my beautiful bride enjoy her anniversary present." He sat down in a wing chair which offered the best view, as Anne asked her Black stud to fuck her again.

Desiree Davidson

Susan's Twister Party

It was time for one of Susan's sex parties. She said it would have a 'twist' when she called me. With Susan in charge that could mean anything. She told me not to bring a date because she would have a girl friend for me. I'd never been disappointed by Susan's selection and I was sure her choice would be perfect. Susan's parties always had a sexual theme and always resulted in four men pairing off with four women and going to their separate bedrooms to spend two hours having sex. Occasionally there was an inter-bedroom swap after the first hour, but all sex was behind closed doors.

I arrived at the party and Susan introduced me to my date for the evening--Sandy Mc…
Sandy was a cute red head and well built. Sandy was a senior at the University of Oklahoma. I fixed some snacks for us and sat down on a couch in the game room with Sandy. After we finished our snacks I began to kiss Sandy gently and romantically but the cute little doll very quickly stepped up the pace to passionate kisses. Her full lips drew me to her. As we kissed I stroked her face and hair and gently explored her legs.

At 8:30 pm Susan left her date's embrace and went to each couple announcing that we were going to play 'Strip 21' for a party game. This was something new. We gathered around her table and she had four decks of cards. Tim and Debbie took turns shuffling and cutting the cards. The rules were simple: the dealer (Susan) dealt two cards to the guest

47

and two to herself. The guest then decided if they would stand pat or make 21 through a third requested card. Susan made the same decision. If Susan won, then the guest had to remove the number of clothes equal to the difference of their hand and 21. This very rapidly left all eight people totally naked. Susan then had each of the girls and guys draw a number to pair us off at random. In our case, Sandy and I ended up together. We and the others proceeded to the couches to continue making out until time was called.

Sandi had large beautiful nipples which got lots of attention from me. She was a real redhead–a pretty matching trim covered her swollen pussy lips. I moved my hand from her soft legs and separated her labia with my fingers and found she was lubricated and totally relaxed. My finger settled on her clit and as we made out I proceeded to bring her to eight orgasms in twenty minutes. As I played with her, she gauged my cock's size and length as she stroked it with her talented hand. Susan called time at the hour. We gathered around again and she announced that one couple was going to play a game called 'Twister' before we went to our bedrooms. To select the couple to play, she had 12 cards and dealt three to each couple. Whoever had high cards would play the game. Sandy and I had a winning hand and everyone else had nothing--I'm sure Susan had stacked the deck to insure Sandy and I were the couple to play the game.

Susan spun the dial around the positions on the game wheel and Sandy and I assumed them on the large colored dots on the plastic sheet on the floor. Our naked bodies made contact as we moved into positions and my cock was hard as rock and was

48

seeping pre-cum. The last spin had Sandy down on her hands and knees and I on my knees immediately behind her. The head of my hard cock actually parted the swollen outer lips of her cunt in this position.

Susan asked, "Sandy do you want to do it?"

Sandy said "Yes!"

Susan asked, "Do you want a condom?"

Sandy said, "No, I want to feel his big cock shoot cum in me."

I immediately placed my hands on Sandy's hips and thrust my cock into her wetness. A roar of approval went up from the other six people and I increased my pace of fucking her. After about five minutes she started coming on me.

When she caught her breath she said, "I want to keep fucking but I want to be on my back." I pulled out of her and a long stream of clear excitement dripped from my unsatisfied cock.

 Her pretty trimmed red bush glistened with our wetness.

Susan brought two quilted comforters and a pillow and Sandy lay down on them. Her beautiful red hair fanned out on the pillow. I leaned over her and kissed her full lips.

I said, "Sandy this is going to be special."
As I looked into her green eyes I positioned myself between her pretty legs and she took hold of my cock and placed the head in her swollen cunt lips. Sandy was really a 'fire cracker' for as I thrust into her she wrapped her legs around my back and came for the second time and kept coming. She was as big an exhibitionist as I.

We continue to fuck for about five minutes when the others began a chant for me to come in her. I did just that, shooting stream after stream of cum into her body. Again she came at the same time, crying out with me as we took each other.

I pulled out of her and was still hard and ready for another go. My white, creamy, cum oozed out of her cunt.

Sandy looked at me and said, "It appears that you are still ready; I am too. I want to ride you." I lay down beside her on my back and Sandy straddled my body and guided my cock back into her wet cunt. In this 'woman astride position' she angled her torso toward my chest maximizing my cock's contact with her clit. The other couples cheered us on as Sandy flexed her legs to rise just so the head of my cock was in her and then thrust all the way down its shaft. She had only been riding me for about three minutes when she began to have chain orgasms, one orgasm after another. This girl was phenomenal. Our watchers were ready to start their own sessions and they began to chant come, come, come, come … As Sandy plunged down on my cock, she said "Now!" and both of us came together.

My cock again filled her pussy with cum. We lay joined for a time as she lay on my chest. Then she lay down beside me and I pulled her to me so I could kiss her and fondle her breasts. Shortly we realized the other six people had gone off to their bedrooms while we remained in each other's arms enjoying the afterglow of sex.

Sandy and I got up and went down the hall to the bedroom with an open door. I led her into the bedroom and we lay down on our sides facing each other. I asked her if I could clean her up and give her a few more orgasms. I lay down on my back with a doubled pillow under my head. Then I asked Sandy to straddle my head. That placed her cunt right over my mouth as she held on to the headboard. I thrust my tongue into her, licking my warm cum from her pussy; then when she was cleaned up, I began to tongue her clit. In just a few minutes she began to have chain orgasms again. After about twenty minutes, she moved off me and lay beside me, almost exhausted, but she began fondling my cock and balls as I kissed her and sucked her nipples.

We talked about other things we would like to do with each other. I told her I'd like to 69 with her if my large cock wasn't too uncomfortable for her mouth.

"I'd like to come in your mouth and then French kiss with you and take the cum into my mouth," I said.

She had something else in mind for a grand finale, but first we moved into a 69 position and proceed to lick and fondle each other. Shortly, she placed her lips around the head of my cock and began to suck. With each suck, Sandy pulled more of my big cock into her mouth. As I flicked her clit with my tongue, she proceeded to move her hand up and down on the upper shaft while swirling her tongue over the sensitive parts of the head. She began to come and I began to come. When I finished, I pulled away and moved up to her mouth to receive my cum back in a French kiss. The excess cum dribbled down both our chins due to the copious amount her expert mouth had pulled from my balls. I asked what she wanted to do now; we had about forty-five minutes left of our private party.

Sandy said, "Susan told me you have a selective bisexual side."

"Indeed I do."

"What did you have in mind?"

She said, "The one thing I have never done is to have anal sex."

I said, "Anal sex is both bisexual and heterosexual and I had considerable experience both ways."

She said, "That's what I want, an experienced man who is patient and gentle to introduce her to the act.

I leaned over and kissed her as my hand roamed over her firm breasts and her large nipples.

I always brought a small zippered bag with me when I came to Susan's parties. Inside were large condoms in case a partner didn't want me to come in her, as well as finger condoms, latex gloves, Vaseline and KY Jelly, and hand lotion.

"Sandy do you want me to introduce you bare back or do you want a condom?" I asked.

She said, "You silly man, my cunt is drenched with your cum and I want my ass to be the same!" I went on and said, "We can do it spooned, you on hands and knees, or us face to face with your legs over my shoulders."

"I suggest the latter," I said, "I want to look into your beautiful green eyes as I fuck you.
It was so easy to bring her to orgasm with vaginal entry; I wanted to see if Sandy would come from having her ass fucked.

I asked her to lie on her side while I gently lubricated her anus and opened her with one finger, two fingers and then three, to make sure she could accommodate me. Then she rolled over and sat up and lubricated the head and shaft of my cock. She then turned on her back. I positioned myself between her beautiful freckled legs and lifted them onto my shoulders. She took my cock and placed it against her little relaxed hole. I eased the head of my cock into her, slowly opening her again as I'd done with my fingers. I stayed there applying steady pressure. As she relaxed I pushed into her past her sphincter muscle.

I asked, "Are you comfortable with my size."

She said, "Yes. Please go slowly."

I asked if I should go on and she said yes and I gently eased my cock into her until I bottomed out and my big balls were against her ass.

I didn't have to ask.

She said, "Fuck me now, I feel like I'm ready to come."

I gave her about a dozen full length strokes and she began to come in those long chain orgasms of hers. Her pulsating canal felt like it was squeezing cum out of me, so I began to shoot streams of cum into this delicious little girl's ass. When I finished filling her with cum I stepped into the bathroom and wet a wash cloth and came out and cleaned Sandy up. Then I went back and urinated and cleaned my cock so it was as clean as at the start of the evening. As I handled my cock to clean it, the texture of the washcloth and the slipperiness of the soap and the use of a towel to rough dry it stimulated me to have another raging hard on. I walked back into the bedroom and Sandy took a turn in the bathroom. When Sandy came back she asked, "How much do you come when you ejaculate?"

53

I said, "Find out."

I got some lotion from my bag and told her to apply it to my cock and jack me off. I lay flat on my back while she sat beside me and stroked my cock with her soft hand. A few minutes passed and I told her I was about to come and she picked up the pace. Suddenly she cried out "Oh my God!"

The first stream of white, creamy, cum shot out of my cock and hit directly in her face; as did the successive shots. Her pretty mouth and nose was covered in cum. There was even a pearl strand in her beautiful, dark red hair.

I sat up and took her into the bathroom and showed her in the mirror the pretty pearl necklace in her hair. Sandy said, "I've never been with anyone who came that much."

I said, "I've met a few others in my life, and I was sure she eventually would meet them too.

I took a fresh washcloth and cleaned her face and wiped the cum out of her hair and. We then returned to the bedroom and lay on the bed on our sides facing each other and talking about how good we were together. We fondled each other for a while, and then returned to long passionate kisses.

Hearing Susan's bell ringing, we got up and dressed and returned to the game room for refreshments before going our separate ways.

Masquerade

I had never been anywhere in South America and my Spanish was rotten, but here I was sitting in Quito, Ecuador. I'd be here for a month to manage the native engineers in designing an electrical variable speed driver pump station to be added to the Trans-Andean Pipeline.

The native engineering manager and I did not hit it off immediately, but when I brought him a painting after visiting a 'crafts' fair, everything was cool. I had noted his computer's screen saver was a pretty naked senorita lying back on a huge motorcycle; I knew what he would want.

I couldn't give him a motorcycle or the senorita, but I brought him a painting of a beautiful senorita lying on a backdrop, wearing a festival mask so the upper portion of her face was covered and all she had on were knee high, green socks. I handed the package to him and on tearing open the paper, he was so excited he was immediately looking for a hammer to hang the painting on his wall.

I was watching him hang it when Mercedes, the 23 year old Office Manager, handed me several papers to sign. She was very close showing me where to sign

She said quietly, "The painting is nice, but I'd look better in that costume."
I stood up as she did and I handed the papers back to her and our hands accidentally touched.
I looked directly into her dark green eyes and said "I would very much like to see her in that pose."

Mercedes was a doll. She was about 5'3" and had naturally curly black hair that she wore down around her shoulders. She was of slim build, but she had large 'D-Cup' breasts. She was wearing a thin cotton dress blouse and a short yellow skirt that accented every curve... She was a living doll.

A few days later my driver was sick and Mercedes came to pick me up at my hotel in the morning. As she drove away I noted she had on dark green knee high socks.

"Was it possible?" I thought.

The day went quickly and Mercedes came to my office to see if I was ready to go. I told her I would be just a minute, to sit down. She had on a short skirt about nine inches above the knee and the skirt was a plaid and its short length highlighted her green stockings. She was wearing a matching plaid vest over a white eyelet blouse. She really looked great! Soon, I was logged off and locked up and ready to go. We went to the parking garage and climbed into her vehicle and she headed out to my Hotel.

"Mercedes," I said, "Will you join me for dinner?"

Mercedes agreed and went up to my room so I could take a quick shower. I was certain I was going to have this little South American doll, but I didn't know how--I couldn't read her face or eyes--I didn't have to.

Mercedes came up to my room to see if the company was getting the room the hotel was charging her for. She asked to use the bathroom. Then when she came out I went in and took my shower. As I dried myself I was oozing pre-cum. Mercedes asked me to come out and I wrapped a towel around my waist. When I came out Mercedes was on my bed and was in the pose of the painting I had given Carlos. She was beautifully naked except for her green stockings and the festival mask covering her eyes and nose.

Mercedes said, "What do you think, Eric, am I better than the painting?"

I said, "You're much better; you are beautiful and fully alive!"

Mercedes told me to take my towel off and sit down on the couch. I did and she came to me and knelt in front of me. Her breasts were beautiful and begging to be touched.

Mercedes touched my fully erect cock and said, "I see the other girls in our office building have not been lying.

"Am I too late to get the best treatment?" she asked.

"You are not too late--you are just in time-- please help yourself," I said.

Mercedes took my cock in her delicate hand and began to tongue its head. She still had on the mask and it made it even more exciting to have her licking and sucking me incognito. She mastered taking me and in a few minutes she had me coming in her mouth. She rose up to me and with her hard nipples thrust into my chest, she French kissed me and gave me back my cum. She then led me by the hand to the king sized bed. We lay down and kissed for awhile and I asked to take her mask off.

She said, "It is not permitted."
I moved between her legs and found her firm clit with my tongue and very quickly brought her to long strings of orgasm. When I moved away she reached

down and pulled me up on top of her. The sexy masked girl was a little tight for entry for my over sized cock, but shortly she opened like a flower and I penetrated her fully. We fucked for fifteen minutes and she was coming practically all the time. Then I came and filled her tight little pussy with my semen. She said, "Oh damn, my diaphragm slipped off when you were thrusting so deep.

I said, "Don't worry I'm a safe play toy, I had a vasectomy thirteen years ago.

She seemed relieved. We sixty-nined and then fucked again. She was wonderful. She got up from the bed and went to the rest room and when she returned, she still had her mask on. She dressed with it on and I dressed as well.

When she was fully dressed, she kissed me and asked me to take the mask off. I did and as it cleared her face she said, "Senor Eric I will ask the hotel to make some adjustments for your comfort."

It was a very clear signal that all between us was private and without the mask she was the Office Manager. I kept the mask and had the pretty little girl over six times before I headed back to the United States. She was more playful each time and was my best memory of Quito, Ecuador.

Desiree Davidson

Naughty or Nice

At the beginning of our marriage Eric, you suggested a threesome as an introduction to my expanded sex life.

I was teaching high school English and there was this man English teacher who challenged my academics and the morals I was attempting to incorporate in my lessons. For some reason he was very hot to me, maybe it was because he contended with me over everything. I told you about him, and you began to tease me that he was the one for my first experience. I resisted, but my resolve wavered; I found myself turned on all day and looking forward to talking to him after school, and yes flirting with him when he would stop by my classroom at the end of the day. School ended at 3 and you got home after 6:30 pm consistently and many times he and I would talk forever."

You teased me and encouraged me and one day I came home with a few things from the drug store, and there was a box of condoms. I had decided and they went in my purse, but they were never used. Before I put them away, you held them up and said, "Just so you'll know, these are worthless, manufacturers don't make one big enough for Stan." You said, "You'll just have to take him bareback like you have me for the 4 years you've been off birth control pills. If he impregnates you, it's no big deal-- we'll have the baby we've been wanting." I was not the least put off by what you said, and over the next week I became more seductive in my flirting. I talked

59

to you about wanting to be alone at first and then have you join in, and you supported everything I wanted and encouraged my determination.

The following Saturday, we went to Oklahoma City and bought new beautiful sheer lingerie, garter belt and stockings. The panties had ribbon ties at the sides, so they could be removed without removing anything else. The bra had front closure. You bought a beautiful silk cream blouse, low cut and button down the front. A pretty pastel blue mini skirt coordinated with the lingerie. The pastel blue high, high heels which matched a new hand bag, coordinated with everything. When you put it on at home with your pale pink choker pearls you were a living doll!

Monday, there was nothing. Tuesday there was nothing. Wednesday there was nothing, and then Thursday came and I was dressed for a seduction. Eric, I went to school with the intent of seducing him. As it turned out the seduction was more a mutual agreement thing. School ended and Stan came into my room, he closed the door and locked it. The blinds were down and we were alone. He walked over to my chair. As he approached, he told me how beautiful I looked in the new outfit. He stood by my chair. I could see Stan's huge erection outline and as he slid his hand into my bra and cupped my breast, I reached for his erection. He removed his hand, lifted me up and kissed me passionately several times. He told me he wanted me, and I confirmed I wanted him. What happened next surprised me. Luckily there was nothing breakable on my desk, for he swept everything off. He laid me down on the desk. I thought condom–then I realized he was even bigger

than you Eric. I had been wet all day and I was ready!
He slowly un-buttoned my blouse and opened my
front close bra exposing my breasts, he lifted me and
slid my mini skirt up around my waist, pulled the
ribbons on my panties and exposed me completely,
then he dropped his pants and shorts and there was
that beautiful, huge, throbbing cock. He opened my
lips and placed the huge head against my cunt. He
leaned over and kissed me and played with my
breasts until I asked him to please fuck me hard and
fast, or I might change my mind. We came together
and he filled me with his cum. Because this was
forbidden sex, it was more intense than with you
Eric. Stan asked if I wanted to continue and I said
yes, Eric won't be home till 9 tonight.
We put ourselves back together and I took him home
to our bed. We didn't know what time was and it
seemed like we made love forever. The sex was
beautiful and he held me and caressed me after each
time. He was a romantic at heart and I loved the
things he said to me. After our sixth intercourse, he
told me this would have to be our last, but only for
now. Eric, you told me we were so enraptured with
each other that during the sixth time we made love,
you actually walked into the hall by our bedroom's
open door, and watched our last time, for it was after
nine. Stan left me with a long passionate kiss. I could
hardly let him go. I was lying naked on the bed,
Stan's huge amount of semen back flowing out of
me, when you walked in and stripped off your
clothes, as you asked if I had a good time.

"I wanted to shout to the world I had his big
cock and I had orgasms before, but these were
orgasms! He took me like I had never been taken," I

61

thought. There was no way to answer your question fully, so I said softly, "Yes!"

You slipped in to our bed beside me and kissed me and told me you loved me and you'd like details. Eric you asked me to kneel above your head so you could lick my lover's cum from my thoroughly dilated vagina and I told you all Stan and I did, from the classroom to the final. We finished in more ways than one and were lying together facing.

You were prepared for my question, Stan and you had talked as he left and the two of you had already agreed if I wanted it.

"Eric," I said, "I want to be with my Stan again--alone--as soon as possible."

You said, "He'll pick you up here Friday after school and take you to his home for the weekend, and his girl friend Susan or 'Wild Thing' as I came to christen her, would spend the weekend with me, Eric. We agreed this was what we wanted, and the swap is what happened, for that first weekend and a significant number after.

There were many times we had that threesome we had initially planned, but as the months progressed, you told me you enjoyed watching us two as much as you enjoyed doubling me. You told me I was so beautiful and totally responsive with him. You said you had never seen anyone have the intensity of orgasms with him that I had with him. He seemed to know exactly what I needed and could deliver it. You told me that we were the most perfectly sexually matched couple you had ever seen.

Christmas came and you planned a surprise for me. I bought you an electric train that year, because I kept 'remembering' my child-hood train. You had bought me a sexy lingerie outfit and matching high-high heels. It was pale mist blue. It consisted of a little string ribbon tie sheer jacket falling just below my breasts, the French cut panties were also ribbon tie at the sides, the garter belt and hose were a perfect match to the bra and bikini. I asked you to open your gift first, and you told me it was just what you'd had when you were a boy. Then I opened mine. You asked me to go to our bedroom and put it on and then let you see me by the Christmas tree.

You said Stan had been waiting in our dark kitchen and quickly came out, stark naked with a huge erection from just from hearing my pretty voice and the anticipation of having all of you. You quickly tied six ribbons at two inch intervals, each with a bell on his erect cock. He stood just in the darkness of the kitchen off the dining room where we had the Christmas tree. I came back to the tree and you told me I was a vision of sexual excitement.

You said that you had another gift and came to me and kissed me until Stan could be standing behind me.

We finished the kiss, you quickly moved aside as I opened my eyes and saw Stan.

You said "I'm giving you your lover for Christmas.'"

He stepped to me and took me in his arms and I kissed him and I touched the bells and ribbons and asked, "What are these for? Do they have a purpose?"

You said they do and Stan kissed me as he slipped the ribbons loose on the jacket and took the jacket off exposing my beautiful breasts to his hands and mouth.

63

Desiree Davidson

You untied the ribbons at the panties sides and my lover, and your fellow 'Hunter' picked me up in your stockings and high heels and carried you to our bed and lay you down.

You told me that you had never seen any woman lubricate and relax so fast, as Stan positioned above me, I placed him for entry and he slid in two inches. You removed a belled ribbon, he went four; we proceeded as you told me at each bell ring, his next 2 inches was another gift from you. When you removed the sixth, you told me how much you loved me, and you said you wanted only the best sexual partner for me. I was with him many times before, but as Stan fully penetrated me with 14 thick inches, you said that we were so beautiful together and I came solely on the gentle slow penetration and your words. You kissed me, told me he was all mine, and I was all his, and to enjoy myself. You said you would be sleeping in the bedroom across the way. I wrapped my stocking covered legs around Stan's back and held him to receive his last streams of come. You told me that seeing my pretty heels on his back was so erotic. As we made love, you watched us through the open doors, and you set up your train. You said that seeing the two of us and hearing the sounds of sex and the beautiful sounds of the two of us coming was fantastic.

We had threesomes, but as a couple Stan and I had the greatest joy in sex. Our relationship continued into the fall, when you accepted a job with Mobil in Dallas. While you were away, Stan came to our home many times, and we never stopped until the moving van pulled away when school ended for me.

64

Desiree Davidson

Birthday Sex with Strangers

It was February and for my birthday on the 13th I usually try to treat myself to a sex party and see how many partners I can have in eight hours.

When I was waiting in the bar for my table, I met a woman named Charlotte. She was an attractive blond and was sporting some very pretty breasts as shown by her low cut blouse. I was 51 years old today and I never got tired of pursuing a new sexual encounter. Charlotte would be number 5121 in my sexual inventory. I invited her to dinner and she was a sparkling companion. We had a good time getting to know each other. It was obvious she was going to give me a birthday surprise on this Tuesday night. After dinner she took me back to her apartment and we had a fun time of sexual entertainment. It lifted my spirits because my work assignment was three weeks long and I did not get to go home on the weekends to my wife, Desiree.

Charlotte invited me to stay the night and she so enjoyed me she invited me to stay with her through Friday night. When I came in on Friday, she said she had a belated birthday surprise for me--we were going to a sex party that night.

I had been to many sex parties, so the expanse of naked flesh was not surprising to me.

I asked Charlotte what she would like to do before we split up for the evening. Charlotte answered by going and getting a man that appealed to her. She wanted to impale her delicious ass on Loren, lay back on his chest and let me take her pussy for a double penetration. That is exactly what she did and the naughty little girl started coming shortly after my first entry.   Charlotte was primed for the rest of the party. I might be 51 years old but I still recover quickly, and very shortly I found myself standing in line to gang bang a babe named Alexis.

Alexis was a fiery red head and when I entered her cum soaked pussy I looked into her green eyes and fucked her hard and fast and added my cum to that of the seven men who fucked her before me while I watched.

I went from Alexis and moved to Hope. She was an attractive blonde haired, green eyed, sexy bitch. She took me woman astride and I played with her small, firm breasts the whole time she rode me. When she would come her stiff nipples would soften and then recover their hardness. She rode for about 15 minutes and my cock exploded in her tight cunt and filled her with my cum.

Next I moved to Cassandra. She was about 36 and had beautiful large breasts. She also took me women astride and again I had her delicious breasts to play with the whole time she rode me. I lasted about twenty minutes before I flooded her with cum. I was slowing down in recovery so I switched and found a male friend.

Eric had a muscular build and a seven inch, medium thickness, cock. He had sandy brown hair and he told me he was 44 as we discussed him fucking me in the ass. He entered me and my cock instantly came erect. He felt good and I concentrated on his rhythm and felt the swell of his cock as he began to shoot his cum in my ass.

I was about to go back to the women when James asked if he could suck me off. We lay on our sides and I thrust my cock into his mouth. He was a handsome man with black wavy hair and grey eyes. He had very little hair on his body--unlike my bear-like, hairy body. When I came in his mouth I gagged him with my copious cum but he managed to take it all. James sucked me hard again and I wanted a woman.

I saw Connie a slim little girl with pert B-cup breasts. She was 37 and after fucking her face to face, I sucked and licked her pussy and brought her to a number of oral orgasms to complement the ones she had while I was fucking her. She sucked me hard again and I moved over to her friend Regina.

Regina was a red headed doll with firm D-cup breasts. She was 33 and had never had children and her breasts showed it--they were perfect. I positioned Regina on her hands and knees and as I fucked her I reached under and cupped her breasts. That brought her off like a fire cracker and her pussy did its best to milk me dry.

She took the stiffness out of me and I was flaccid for about 30 minutes so I found Rosemarie and Amanda and got them off with my tongue. Both of them sucked my partially flaccid cock and Amanda brought me to full stiffness again. Another man was waiting to be with her, so I moved on to Donna.

Donna was a real red head complete with green eyes and freckles. I kissed all over her body exploring the freckles and then I mounted her and fucked her face to face. She came easily and the greedy, little, bitch just kept coming. After about ten minutes I cut loose and shot stream after stream of cum into her pretty red haired pussy. I talked to her awhile and it turned out it was her birthday too, she was 31 years old. Since I had already given her my best, I offered her long passionate kisses and gave her the best kisses of all and stimulated her clit with my tongue until she could hardly stand the intensity of her orgasms. I might have fucked her again but Loren was waiting to fuck her.

I moved on to Pamela and I was wiped out in the cum and erection departments and I spent a long time just giving her oral sex while I recuperated. I wanted to end the party on an up note. I had recovered while I was with Pamela and I invited Cassandra to straddle my face while Abby sucked me off. The three of us were coming together in no time.

Not counting Charlotte since she came with me, I had sex with 13 new partners I knew nothing about. It was a rush to have un-protected sex with 3 men and 11 women in a space of about 8 hours.

I gathered up Charlotte and we went to her apartment and made love in the shower. It was a wonderful birthday gift!

Desiree Davidson

Got a Minute?

I saw her leave the Thai Embassy and cross the street and head toward the park. She was headed right for me. She was a doll. The weather was mild in Hong Kong with just a tinge of coolness. Rachel was wearing a white linen blouse and a red 'Scottish' plaid skirt which ended about six inches above her knees. She was wearing black, high-heeled boots and red stockings. I heard the tap, tap, tap, of her heels on the park sidewalk. I had to act quickly. I headed up the sidewalk and noted she was wearing a watch.

I said, "Got a minute, do you have the time?"

She stopped and said it was 11:33.
I fiddled with my watch and as I did it, I said, "Hi, I'm Eric, you have a beautiful 'Aussie' accent." I paused for her to fill in her name.

"Rachel," she said "Rachel."

"What a lovely name you have, Rachel," I said.

"Rachel", I said, "I just got off my ship--I'm in the U.S. Navy--and have never been here before, so can you tell me a good place to have lunch?"

She said," Yes, I'm headed to a restaurant on the other side of the park; why don't you join me."

I walked with her through the park and found out she was an English teacher specializing in taking one who has learned formal English and teaching them to relax their formal speech and that included their gaining an understanding of idioms and slang of the language."

"It makes the speaker relaxed and more real," she told me.

Desiree Davidson

Rachel and I had lunch and all during lunch, she was asking me about American idioms and American slang usage. She was working with the Thai Ambassador and had been for two weeks getting him ready to meet with the American Ambassador and the British Ambassador. He wanted to fit in instead of sounding like a parrot. Language improvement tutoring was how she made her living.

I asked, "How did you end up in Hong Kong?" Rachel said, "I followed my fiancée here and I caught him in bed with a Chinese girl young enough to be his daughter, so the planned wedding was off, but I decided to stay anyway."

"At first I taught school," She said, "But soon I found tutoring paid much more and for far less hours. I did get married but he's on a trip to London." She continued to ask me about American idioms and slang and I continued to think of them.

Rachel said, "You know I have the whole afternoon available. Why don't you come to my apartment and let me tape record your examples."

I was ready and willing--my cock had been hard since I heard the tap, tap, tap of her boots heels. She navigated some 10 blocks and we came to an apartment building. She guided me to her apartment and we set about drinking cokes and recording examples of slang and idioms.

She was beautiful. She had sparkling grey eyes set in a beautiful face framed by lovely black hair flipped under at her shoulders. Her lipstick coordinated with the red of her plaid outfit and made her lips inviting. The red contrasted with the white of her long sleeved blouse which revealed the form of her C-cup breasts. Yes, Rachel was quite beautiful.

70

"Why don't we take a break?"

For the first time, she sat down in an easy chair across from mine. She must have noticed the bulge in my pants giving her the best compliment of all. I could now see much of her legs as she sat in the chair and they were excellent.

"I'm honored to be in the home of such a beautiful woman," I said.

Before she could protest I stood and covered the short distance between us, and was helping her to her feet. I kissed her and she kissed back.

"Can you stay longer? William and I have an open marriage," she said.

I answered, "I have a 72 hour liberty and I am at your disposal any time you want me."

She turned her face up to kiss me and our greedy mouths met. I picked her slender frame up and carried her to her bedroom and we lay on the bed for a long time passionately kissing.

Finally, Rachel said, "Will you make love to me, I haven't had anyone in two weeks and you look like the man I want to end my dry spell."

I kissed her and asked how she wanted me to make love to her.

Rachel said, "Let's start with 'missionary' and see where it leads."

We stood up and undressed each other. She had beautiful breasts crowned with large pink nipples which were very sensitive to the touch of my fingers, lips and tongue. The areolas crinkled and bumped as I ran my tongue around them. She was hard and excited. I touched her pretty mound of dark curly hair and found a wet slit waiting for me.

I placed Rachel on the bed and positioned myself between her legs; she took my cock and nestled the head in her lips. I eased in slowly giving her a chance to accommodate my big cock without any discomfort. When she was fully relaxed she took all of me in her and my big balls were resting on her bottom. I began to move and then accelerated thrusts for my Rachel's pleasure Very soon the beautiful little girl was coming on me in wave after wave of orgasms. After about 15 minutes I joined her and filled her cunt with my sperm laden cum.

We lay together for a long time just looking into each other's eyes and enjoying what we be held. Later we would make passionate love in several positions for my beautiful Rachel was greedy for maximizing her pleasure. I stayed the night and then the other two days and nights I had available. Rachel called the Thai Ambassador's secretary and told her she was ill and Rachel and I had nothing other to do than make loves on those three days!

Desiree Davidson

Come With Me

It was a nice restaurant in the old part of Austin, Texas which at the time had become quite chic. The couple had been seated just after I was seated. I had already noticed her in the waiting area. She was a beautiful blonde, slim with a firm beautiful ass and full C-cups. She was wearing a short yellow dress with spaghetti straps--almost a sun dress--the weather was un-seasonably warm. She had on light green high heels and no stockings were visible. She looked to be about 28. She had a pretty tan. He was dressed in casual clothes, slacks and a polo shirt and brown loafers. By chance, they were seated at a table angled just so I could see them both. I guessed they were married to each other from their rings and how they responded to each other. There appeared to be an element of hostility between them.

I was dressed much like the man except my shirt was blue instead of green. I was out looking for a meal, but I was also looking for a filling dessert of a beautiful woman to make love to.

The thought came to mind I had never tried getting a woman to follow me away from her husband. The more I thought about it, the more I liked the risk and I selected it as my sexual adventure for the evening.

The rib eye steak I ordered and the 'fixings' were delivered in short order. The couple I was interested in was having salad and smaller cut steaks. I hurried through my meal and ordered coffee and paid the bill.

73

I watched the couple the whole time I ate classifying them for a proper approach in this new adventure. Of the pair the woman was dominating. In my mind I was already making her mine.

The couple was within five minutes of finishing their meal when I went over to the beautiful blonde and whispered in her ear, "Leave him for tonight--teach him a lesson for what he's done, you're too beautiful for him, come with me and I will give you a sexual experience you'll never forget. Now get up and tell him you're going with me and I'll bring you home in four hours; you will be perfectly safe."

The blonde got up and whispered to him exactly what I had told her and then she walked out hand-in-hand with me. Her husband never moved and sat there stunned.

I put her in my car and drove to my hotel. She was laughing in the excitement of actually doing what I told her and it working. I was pretty pleased too, I had her.

I'm Janelle," she said, "I never dreamed I would go with a man who asked me on the spur of the moment."

As we parked I asked her if she was sure she wanted to have sex with me. She confirmed she was. I leaned over and kissed her gently and then we kissed with more passion.

"Let's go," she said.

I opened my door and went around the car and opened Janelle's door and caught a glimpse of her beautiful legs. I took her hand and led her to my room.

My hotel had turn down service so the bed had already been turned down. The room was large enough to have a small love seat and one wing back chair. I directed her to the love seat and we began kissing and I fondled her breasts through the sheer fabric of her dress. Her nipples were large and easily excited. The feel of her lightly tanned satin smooth legs was wonderful.

I walked to the bed and took the two chocolates the maid had left on the pillow and returned to the love seat. I gave her a chocolate from my pillow and asked her if she would show me her charms for a chocolate.

"Give me both of them," she teased, "and I will give you me!"

We struck a deal as I handed over the second chocolate.

Janelle stood up and un-zipped her dress and let it fall to the floor. She stood before me with bare breasts, panties and high heels.

I said, "You can take the panties off but I want you to keep your pretty high heels on."
In the soft lamp light I could see that although her mons was closely cropped, my pretty baby was a natural blonde.

She came to me and I took her in my arms and kissed her several times. For the third time I asked her if she was sure she wanted to make love with me.

"Yes, I want you," she replied.

I placed her on the bed. She watched as I removed my clothes. When I was fully naked I could no longer conceal my big cock. It was throbbing against my flat belly and ready to have this lovely dessert. Janelle took me in her hand as I stood by the bed and then she invited me to fuck her. I moved between her legs and with one finger, then two, then

75

three in her wet cunt. I determined she was ready and relaxed. She took my cock in her hand and guided me into her cunt. What a marvelous cunt she had, she tightened her muscles and it was obvious she knew her technique well. I moved completely into her and allowed her to get accustomed to my size and then we began a twenty minute fuck. Janelle was highly orgasmic and she came for several minutes as she cried out, "Oh God! You feel so good…that's it keep fucking me harder!"

Eventually I could not resist having my dessert and as I cried out in ecstasy I shot streams of creamy cum into her. When we finished, I immediately moved into a 69 position so she could lick my cock and I could lick my cum out of her pussy and tongue her pink clit. This brought us to beautiful simultaneous orgasms. Then we lay in each other's arms.

We lay resting for a time but continued to touch faces, lips, breasts and cock and cunt as we enjoyed just being with each other. Janelle told me her favorite position was woman astride and she would like to do that with me. I said that would be wonderful. Then I noted the time and realized we had been having our private party for three hours since we left the restaurant. I asked Janelle how long it would take to get to her place--she said they lived out by the lake; so it would take an hour to get there. I told her to call her husband and tell him she was having such a great time she had decided to spend the night. I laughed as the horny little nymph came back into my arms. I asked her what he said--all he said was I'll expect you in the morning.

Janelle, my special sexual adventure, continued into the early morning. Eventually she slept. I held her as she went to sleep. I did not sleep, for when I feel like I felt that night I never need sleep and I never get tired and with a continual adrenal rush my body goes sexually for days. In the early sunrise, she stirred awake and she called me back into her body for another session of beautiful sex. Janelle was a living doll who liked everything I liked. I did take her home and her husband was already gone for the day, so we made love one last time in her own bed.

Desiree Davidson

Deserved Discipline

When I came back from Vietnam my wife and I rented an apartment just across from the beach. The apartment complex had a 'live in' leasing agent named Christian. The first time I ever met her I wanted her. Desiree and I had lived there about three months when I had my opportunity.

It was Saturday and Christian was in her apartment. I had stopped by her apartment several times with requests for small repairs that were needed. I came to know her a little bit during these visits. She liked to be complimented and she liked flirtatious compliments. Also, she was going to Norfolk Community College to get a certificate in real estate management so the management company she worked for would give her a larger complex to manage. She loved to be asked about that.
One Saturday I dropped by just to talk--no repairs this time--and she was bored--no one had stopped in all day to look at the two apartments she had available. These apartments were nicely furnished. One of the floor plans was a larger unit than the one Desiree and rented. I asked Christian to show it to me. She got her keys and we went to building "A" of the complex. Desiree was taking a Saturday afternoon nap and I was free for a couple of hours.

It was a beautiful large apartment being shown by a beautiful blue eyed blonde with lightly tanned skin. She had told me she went down to the beach when she could.

I sat down on the bed in the apartment and she set down with me.

She said, "What do you think?"

I replied, "I think you are beautiful and I would like to make love to you."

She could see I was excited for my erect cock was trapped down my right pant's leg and was making quite a bulge. There was no need for a seductive approach, for I had been prepping her for this moment for several weeks. It was almost 4 pm when she would end showing apartments and she sat down by me on the bed.

Christian said, "I excite you don't I Eric?" She went on, "Every time I see you, you have an erection. Do I excite you that much?"

"Beautiful Lady," I said, "I even wake up from dreaming about you and every time I have an erection. I want you!"

Christian said, "Eric, you turn me on too, I like how tall you are and your jet black hair and the outline in your pants of a big cock. I want to make love to you too."

She led me back to her apartment and into her bedroom. She was wearing a beach cover-up. She had told me she was planning to go to the beach when she closed leasing at 4:00 pm. She turned her bed down as I stood looking at her pretty body. She had long shapely legs--she was about 5'8", 130 pounds. On the whole, she was quite beautiful. Christian took off her beach cover up and beneath it she was wearing a skimpy bikini bottom and a more ample top for she was a D-Cup. I went to her and took her bikini top off--she had beautiful breasts and at age 25 they were very firm and down-right pert! I removed the bottom of the bikini by pulling the tie strings at the sides and removed it from her body. She was everything I imagined her to be. I had removed my clothes while she was turning down the bed. Now the two of us were naked. We moved onto her bed and began to kiss.

Christian asked, "Eric, how long have you wanted me?"

I answered, "Since the day I leased our apartment I've wanted you. I want you most right now though!"

We began to kiss and fondle each other. She was fascinated by the size of my cock, and I was fascinated by her beautiful, big, firm breasts and huge nipples.

"What would you like to do?" I asked.
She wanted to try to suck me off. She barely got me in her mouth and the hot little bitch was mostly licking me like a lolly pop when I erupted, shooting streams of come onto her face and breasts as she pushed me down. She was an expert and she felt great. I licked my cum off of her face and breasts and then went and got a warm wash cloth to clean her up. When I came back, I was fully hard again.

Christian and I lay holding and touching and kissing; then she said she wanted me to fuck her. She opened her legs and I moved between them to position on top of her. She took my cock and nestled it in her pussy lips and I exerted firm pressure until her cunt was ready to take me. I entered her slowly and when I was in her completely, I waited for her to adjust to the size of my cock.

Christian told me, "I'm ready; please fuck me now--you feel so good!"

I began to move in her and rapidly built into full thrusting. We fucked about 10 minutes and I began to shoot streams of my white creamy cum into her. When I finished, I collapsed by her and began to pet her anew. I put a doubled pillow under my head and had her straddle my head so I could give her pussy the oral attention she needed to come. I had been licking her clit for about five minutes when she began such intense orgasms that I could hardly keep at her clit as she was moving so much. Finally she said it was enough.

We went in the shower and cleaned the traces of our love making from each other's bodies. She had to go she said, she had to meet her boy friend down by the pier. Neither of us was fully satisfied, but our next liaison would take care of that.

I returned to my apartment and Desiree was still napping, but not for long, I was still hungry for sex and I woke my pretty baby to make love.

On Sunday, Desiree and I had just returned from church and were walking toward our apartment when Christian came out. She was wearing a sheer, yellow, skimpy bikini and she looked good enough to eat. She smiled and said hello as we passed each other. When we got inside, Desiree started to wipe off some dishes for lunch and I was standing right by her.

"You pig" she said, "You thought that slut looked good!" and she slapped me with her damp dish towel.

I laughed and said, "Desiree, you look much better in your bikini than her."

In my mind I thought, "Because Christian looks much better with no bikini!"

Desiree Davidson

A London Delight

Chelsea was the most beautiful of the women I picked up on my trip to London and on to the ancient city of Cairo, Egypt. I saw her walk out of a doorway leading to second floor apartments. She had on black high heels which could be seen as her cute bell bottom jeans swished about her feet. Topping the jeans, she had a white camisole topped by a long red "U" neck sweater with long sleeves coming down onto her hands. She had beautiful long blond hair rolled in long relaxed spirals.

It was crowded at 8 pm in the Piccadilly district of London, and because she was short and thin, I lost her in the crowds. My loss I thought, I would have loved to have met her and killed her softly with kisses and orgasms.

I looked around for about half an hour and I couldn't get the pretty little bell-bottomed clad girl out of my mind.

I decided to have something to eat in a small eatery advertising a special on fish and chips. I went in and placed an order for the 'special' and a Coke. I was looking for a place to sit in the crowded little hole in the wall, when I saw her sitting alone at a table. I walked up to her and asked if I could sit with her. She nodded yes, and I sat down and introduced myself as Eric.

She replied, "I'm Chelsea."

"Are you an American?" she asked, as I looked deeply into her green eyes.

She said, "Tell me about America."

I said, "America is a vast country of 300 million people and over 150 million of them are women, and only a few of them are as beautiful as you, Chelsea!" She had a classically beautiful face and full lips. They were covered in a bright shade of red matching her sweater. We ate our fish and chips and came to know a few things about each other. She told me she was 31 and a bookkeeper and lived just up the street. I told her I was 46 and an electrical engineer and I'm on my way to Cairo, Egypt for a business meeting. She said, "Other than a trip across the channel to Paris I have never traveled."
I told her she was lucky to be at home.

"I was not lucky;" I said, "I have traveled to 20 countries and the District of Columbia and 37 states of the 50 United States in my work."

She said, "I wish I could stay and hear about your travels but I have to call my 'Mum.' I told her I would check in at 9:00 pm and let her know how my new job is going."

Then Chelsea said, "Come with me to my flat and after my call, you can tell me all about your travels."

I went with her. In the US we would call her flat a studio apartment with everything together except the bathroom.

She placed her call at 9 pm. It was interesting to hear her crisp British accent. While she talked, I looked at a magazine and then picked up a book off the floor--a book about modern philosophy. In about 15 minutes, she 'rang off' and came and sat on the arm of the big chair where I was sitting. She looked over my shoulder at what I was reading. I put the book down on the floor where I had found it.

83

Just to see what she would do, I pulled her off the arm and into my lap and kissed her. She kissed back-- always a good sign.

Chelsea was a little girl and fit nicely in my lap. I am 6'2" and of medium build and her weight at about 105 pounds was nothing.

My cock was hard and I'm sure she could feel it against her bottom for she said, "My, you are a ready one!"

I said, "I will always be ready for you." I'm thinking about carrying you over to that bed and getting better acquainted.

Chelsea said, "Let's get better acquainted."

She passionately kissed me again with her full red lips. I stood up taking her with me in my arms, and carried her a few feet to the bed. I lay her down with her feet sticking over the edge of the bed and I removed her cute black patent high heels. I unbuttoned her bell bottom jeans and pulled then from her great looking legs. I sat her up and took her long bright red sweater off and laid it on the chair where I had placed her jeans. I then took her camisole and panties off and I had a beautiful naked lover ready to play.

While I took my clothes off, Chelsea turned down the bed and showed me her beautiful firm ass. She got into bed and I joined her. She turned her back to me and we spooned allowing me full access to her lovely, firm breasts. My cock pressed through her legs and was against her naked blond pussy. I held her and kissed her neck and her beautiful hair. My hands roamed over her firm B-cup breasts and played with her large pink nipples. I told her I wanted to make love to her and she moved onto her back.

I moved on top of her and she took my cock and placed me in her wet pussy lips and I gently eased into her. She was small and tight on my big cock and it felt wonderful. I fucked her with long slow strokes until the pretty baby began to come, each orgasm stronger than the last. We fucked for about 15 minutes and then both of us exploded in climax. I flooded her little body with my creamy white cum and she just kept on coming as I continued to move in her. I was not a young man anymore, but her visual picture below was so stimulating I could stay hard for her to finish. I pulled out of her still mostly hard and she went down on me and left pretty red lipstick marks on my cock as she sucked me totally hard again. She knew how to treat a man's cock. Soon, she had me coming in her mouth and she couldn't take it all, so I shot cum all over her beautiful breasts and then I kissed and licked her breasts.

Chelsea stroked my cock back hard again and she mounted woman astride. The naughty, little, bitch rode me like a rodeo rider on a bucking bronco and again I flooded her pussy with cum. She collapsed in joy onto my hairy chest and her golden blond hair covered me. I asked her if she now had enough of the 'United States?'

She replied, I'm just starting the 'British invasion,' and indeed she engaged me in love making all night long. Starting with a sensuous bath for both of us and long loving sessions through the night, we became one. Our finale was a soft delicious session face to face so I could look into her pretty green eyes as we came with each other.

Desiree Davidson

I woke holding her and I had to rush to the 'tube' (subway) to get back to my hotel and then on to my flight to Cairo out of Heathrow.

Desiree Davidson

A Closer Encounter

Diane and I quickly undressed each other as we stood in my hotel room.

* * *

After all the passengers were all loaded, our aircraft had been disabled when a fuel transfer pump failed in the pilot's check list of critical items. They kept us on the plane for two hours because Portland, Oregon maintenance thought they might be able to fix the problem without replacing the pump. They were wrong and the flight was cancelled.

I was in first class on my way to Seoul, South Korea. Diane was our flight attendant and a great flirt and was quickly moving to the head of my list of people I wished I could be with tonight. Diane was like a sparkling diamond set aflame by pure white light. She had a great personality, intelligence, a powerful sexiness and great looks. I estimated she was in her late twenties. From her banter she knew what she wanted, and if at all possible, I was going to give it to her.

* * *

Diane and I pulled down the bed coverings of the king size bed.

* * *

I had lucked out and was staying at the same hotel as the flight crew and having registered in front of her, I handed Diane my business card. I had written my room number on the back of the card and the words

"You are beautiful--I'd love to show you just how much, Eric."

* * *

I had been in my room only a few minutes when I heard a soft knock on my door. It was Diane. As she came in she handed me my card and said she wanted to cash it in. I took it from her and took her in my arms and kissed her very passionately. After breaking the embrace, we began to undress. The sexual tension was so strong that we jumped onto the bed and we started making out like two teenagers.

My cock slipped into her easily--she was very excited from our flirtation on the plane. When fully in her, I told her how good she felt! I bent down and sucked her nipples--they were about the size of my little finger tip and about a third of an inch when fully erect. She had B-Cup breasts and they were beautiful. As her pussy adjusted, I began to move in a continually more rapid pace. Diane began to come and I helped her on for about ten minutes and then I began to shoot stream after stream of cum into her great little cunt.

When I finished, I moved out of her and saw her neatly trimmed dark red bush dripping with my creamy seed. I held her in my arms and kissed her pretty little freckles. Her shoulder length dark red hair cascaded over the bed pillow. She was a beautiful little sex partner.

Diane was very orgasmic, and I loved to see a woman enjoy sex like she did. We lay and kissed and fondled and in about 15 minutes she was ready to play again. I asked her to take me in the 'woman astride' position. She moved over me and eased down on my long, thick cock. She had a great pussy for extended play; she lubricated easily and remained tight even under significant stretching required to accept me. In short she was fantastic. She rode me like a Wyoming cow girl riding a bucking horse and the intensity of her cries reflected her intense orgasms. She would take me to the edge of coming and I would resist and let her go on her orgasmic way. Finally, I could resist no more and I blasted my seed into her lovely cunt.

Diane collapsed on my hairy chest and fell asleep. I was still hard and I remained in her until she woke in about an hour and had another ride. I was in one of my manic moods again, I didn't need sleep and I was driven to have sex. We played several more hours interspersed with soft touches and passionate kisses. Finally Diane said she had to sleep to be ready for the 16 hour flight tomorrow. I held her as she slept and gently kissed her forehead at her hairline as I stirred her awake at 6 am. She joined me in the shower and we had a fun soapy time followed by the intense stimulation of drying each other. We got dressed and she joined her crew to prepare the plane to receive passengers. We had been in the air about 4 hours when she came and sat in the empty seat next to mine.

Diane whispered in my air, "Are you a member of the mile high club?"

"No," I said.

"Do you want to be?" she said. "If you do, get up and go to the First Class restroom and prepare yourself and I'll be in the galley for a few minutes and then I'll come in and join you," she said.

I did as instructed. Diane came into the rest room. As I sat, my cock was standing at attention in

89

anticipation. Diane pulled her skirt up and her panties aside and settled on my cock. She felt great. I asked her if she had ever had an orgasm this way. She told me no. I replied that things were about to change. She rode me with her back to me and the head of my cock massaged her 'G-spot' until she was coming violently. She was biting her hand to keep from crying out. When I felt she had experienced enough, I shot stream after stream of cum into her fantastic pussy. Diane put herself together and left and spent some time in the galley. I put myself together and I returned to my seat. In a few minutes Diane came and sat in the empty seat beside me. We were softly laughing about the experience. It had been unbelievably hot for both of us.

Diane said, "I think we joined wonderful clubs today--you the mile high and me coming on a big cock for the first time in the air."
Just before we arrived she said, "I have a two day layover in Seoul and I'd love to spend more time with you, Eric."

I said, "I staying at the Renaissance Hotel, and I would welcome your pretty, naked, little body in my bed anytime."

We had a wonderful time those two days and I suppose she left me a gift. When I was getting clothes out of my suitcase a few days later I found in the bottom Delta Gold Wings stamped 'Diane.'

www.ingramcontent.com/pod-product-compliance
Lightning Source LLC
Chambersburg PA
CBHW071243170526
45165CB00003B/1218